Boa Constrictors

by Helen Frost

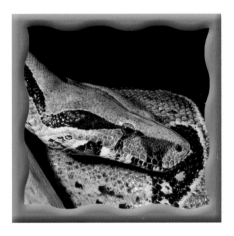

Consulting Editor: Gail Saunders-Smith, Ph.D.

Consultants: The Staff of Black Hills Reptile Gardens,
Rapid City, South Dakota

Pebble Books

an imprint of Capstone Press
Mankato, Minnesota

Pebble Books are published by Capstone Press
151 Good Counsel Drive, P.O. Box 669, Mankato, Minnesota 56002
http://www.capstone-press.com

1 2 3 4 5 6 07 06 05 04 03 02

Library of Congress Cataloging-in-Publication Data
Frost, Helen, 1949–
    Boa constrictors / by Helen Frost.
    p. cm.—(Rain forest animals)
    Includes bibliographical references (p. 23) and index.
    Summary: Simple text and photographs present the lives of boa constrictors that
live in rain forests of South America.
    ISBN 0-7368-1191-5
    1. Boa constrictor—Juvenile literature. [1. Boa constrictor. 2. Snakes.] I. Title.
QL666.O63 F76 2002
597.96′7—dc21   2001004843

Note to Parents and Teachers

The Rain Forest Animals series supports national science standards related to life science. This book describes and illustrates boa constrictors that live in tropical rain forests. The photographs support early readers in understanding the text. The repetition of words and phrases helps early readers learn new words. This book also introduces early readers to subject-specific vocabulary words, which are defined in the Words to Know section. Early readers may need assistance to read some words and to use the Table of Contents, Words to Know, Read More, Internet Sites, and Index/Word sections of the book.

Table of Contents

Boa constrictors are
long, heavy snakes.
Snakes are reptiles.

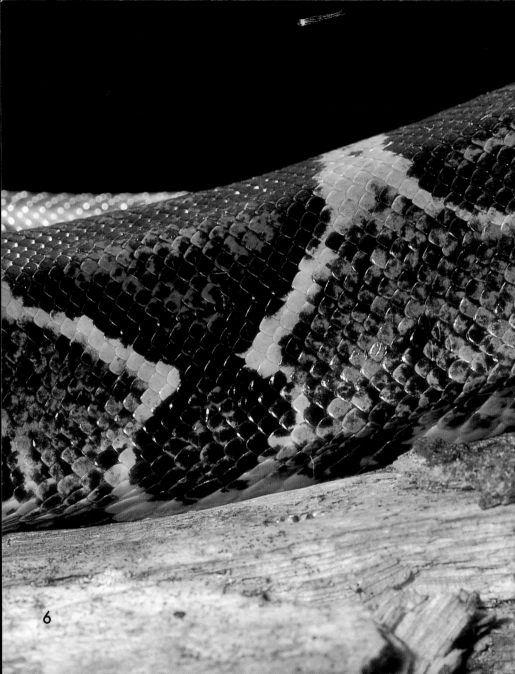

6

Boa constrictors have dark spots or stripes.

tongue →

Boa constrictors have
a tongue.

places boa constrictors live

Most boa constrictors live
in tropical rain forests
from Mexico to
South America.

emergent layer

canopy layer

understory layer

forest floor

Boa constrictors slither mostly along the forest floor. They sometimes climb trees to the canopy layer.

Boa constrictors hunt prey at night. They eat birds, bats, and rats.

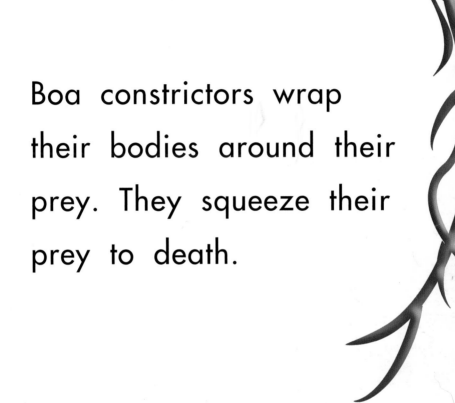

Boa constrictors wrap their bodies around their prey. They squeeze their prey to death.

boa constrictor squeezing a rat

Boa constrictors swallow their prey whole.

boa constrictor eating a rat

Boa constrictors rest
on rocks or in trees.

Words to Know

canopy—the layer of treetops that forms a covering over a rain forest

forest floor—the bottom layer of the rain forest; almost no sunlight reaches the forest floor.

prey—an animal that is hunted by another animal for food; birds, bats, and rats are the prey of boa constrictors.

tropical rain forest—a dense area of trees where rain falls almost every day

reptile—a cold-blooded animal that crawls on the ground or creeps on short legs

slither—to slide along the ground

squeeze—to press something firmly together; boa constrictors squeeze their prey until it cannot breathe.

swallow—to make food or drink travel from the mouth to the stomach; boa constrictors can open their mouths very wide; they can swallow prey whole.

Read More

Chinery, Michael. *Predators and Prey.* Secrets of the Rainforest. New York: Crabtree, 2000.

Dollar, Sam. *Boa Constrictors.* Animals of the Rain Forest. Austin, Texas: Raintree Steck-Vaughn, 2001.

Schlaepfer, Gloria G., and Mary Lou Samuelson. *Pythons and Boas.* Remarkable Animals. Parsippany, N.J.: Dillon Press, 1999.

Internet Sites

Animal Diversity Web—Boa Constrictor
http://animaldiversity.ummz.umich.edu/
accounts/boa/b._constrictor$narrative.html

Boa Constrictors
http://www.enchantedlearning.com/subjects/
reptiles/snakes/boa.shtml

Tropical Rain Forest Animals
http://www.ran.org/kids_action/s2_animals.html

Index/Word List

bats, 15
birds, 15
bodies, 17
canopy
  layer, 13
death, 17
eat, 15
forest
  floor, 13
heavy, 5

hunt, 15
Mexico, 11
night, 15
prey, 15,
  17, 19
rain forest, 11
rats, 15
reptiles, 5
rest, 21
snakes, 5

South
  America, 11
spots, 7
squeeze, 17
stripes, 7
swallow, 19
tongue, 9
trees, 21
whole, 19
wrap, 17

Word Count: 90
Early-Intervention Level: 13

Editorial Credits
Martha E. H. Rustad, editor; Jennifer Schonborn, production designer and interior illustrator; Linda Clavel and Heidi Meyer, cover designers; Kia Bielke, interior illustrator; Kimberly Danger and Mary Englar, photo researchers

Photo Credits
Digital Visions, 10
James P. Rowan, 1
Joe McDonald/TOM STACK & ASSOCIATES, 8, 14
McDonald Wildlife Photography/Joe McDonald, 4, 6, 16, 18, 20
Visuals Unlimited/Joe McDonald, cover

The author thanks the children's section staff at the Allen County Public Library in Fort Wayne, Indiana, for research assistance.